THIS BOOK BELONGS TO JONATHAN BROCK

"on the steps of the Erectheon"   Photograph by Patricia Brock 1969

BRITISH STEAM
1948-1955

Gresley Class A4 4-6-2 No 60013 *Dominion of New Zealand*, in BR blue livery, approaching Potters Bar station, at the summit of the 1 in 200 gradient, with the 4.20pm Sunday Leeds and Bradford express from Kings Cross on September 10, 1950.

E. D. BRUTON

BRITISH STEAM
1948-1955

LONDON

IAN ALLAN LTD

DEDICATION

This album is dedicated to my friend and former colleague, Thomas H. Watts, who made his mark as an Ian Allan railway photographic competition prize winner around 1949, in gratitude for considerable guidance during my early days of learning darkroom technique and of striving for quality.

A down Class C express freight train is seen on the Teignmouth sea wall just west of 'Splash Point' headed by 'Hall' class 4-6-0 No 6907 *Davenham Hall* on Thursday, June 2, 1949.

First published 1976

ISBN 0 7110 0668 7-2/75

Published by Ian Allan Ltd, Shepperton, Surrey, and printed in the United Kingdom by Ian Allan Printing Ltd.

Introduction

In my school and apprenticeship days I had a keen interest in railways, both prototype and model. It was not long before this developed into great admiration for the beautiful action train photographs in the railway journals of the day, the work of the great cameramen of the 1920s and 1930s. I determined that one day I would put the railway as effectively on film. But the warclouds were gathering. Many years were to pass before I could take up lineside photography as a hobby in its own right.

I made a modest beginning in 1946, when my old box and folding cameras were superseded by a second-hand Voigtlander Brilliant 120-size roll film camera. This had a nice f4·5 Skopar lens, although its use on moving subjects was limited by the top speed of 1/300 sec exposure of its Compur shutter. Nevertheless, it produced some promising results and gave me a grounding in the essentials of darkroom practice, both in negative processing and enlarging.

My next venture was the purchase of an old Voigtlander Avus 2½in by 3½in plate camera with three single-sided dark slides. Although it was not much use for fast-moving main-line trains, it gave me valuable experience in handling glass plates, both in changing bag and open dish development in the dark room. I was quickly won over by the superior flatness of the plate compared to the lie of the film in a roll-film camera. By then, too, I had joined Maurice Earley's Railway Photographic Society. So now I gave thought to the acquisition of a press camera suitable for normal express train speeds.

Following correspondence with Maurice Earley on camera types, it became evident to me that the choice lay between the waist-level reflex type as used by Maurice himself (and others) and eye-level press camera as used by Eric Treacy, for example. I had ruled out 'going 35mm', so plate camera it was to be. I sold my model railway 4mm scale layout towards the end of 1947 and a visit to London produced from the proceeds a nice second-hand Zeiss Contessa Nettel press camera in 2½in by 3½in plate size, fitted with a lovely f4·5 Carl Zeiss Jena Tessar lens and a focal plane shutter scaled to 1/1200 sec at the fastest setting.

In the meantime, thanks to the kindness of a friend at the office (a fellow draughtsman), I had learned the secrets of the dark room previously mentioned, including that of striving for print quality. I was now ready to record, process and enlarge anything that the railways at the close of 1947 could present. My emphasis was usually on the pictorial side with, wherever possible, a nice or interesting background, not too much 'clutter' behind the locomotive and the latter clean or reasonably so and putting up a good exhaust, white or black. So up-gradients were preferred to downhill as a locale, although the latter was not ignored. Bridges, signals, etc., were included to add interest when these enhanced the setting. The roll-film cameras (other types of 2¼in square ones were later tried out) were normally used for purely record shots of rolling stock, signals, bridges, etc., of which many were taken for model railway purposes.

By early 1948 I had got to know the press camera, which was put to work on the new British Railways scene following nationalisation on January 1, 1948. It was obvious from the start that the purchase was a lucky one — Jena works Tessars were reputedly the best — and there was now a possibility that my ultimate aim might be achieved.

It was generally claimed by the membership of the Railway Photographic Society that they were photographers first and railway enthusiasts second, but in my mind certainly this was not true. The camera was a means to an end already stated. The success of this exercise must be left to the judgement of the readers for, as an engineering drawing can be 'read', so can a photograph!

The selection of shots finally chosen to illustrate these years of British Railways steam are from a series of negatives exposed between early 1948 and March 1956. It is all too brief a period on reflection, yet one which was full of interest. Here was the new regime in shiny new paint and lettering, yet there a scene which could easily date back to the 1930s or earlier, so unchanged were the motive power, stock and setting.

I followed no set pattern, although favourite locations only a bicycle- or moped-ride from home are evident. Hence, the bulk of the collection is LMR- and ER (GN Section)-oriented. Holidays during the period 1948-1954 were very much arranged with lineside activities in view, especially after 1949 when three visits to the North, each of at least a fortnight's duration, were made in consecutive years. Other odd visits were made on a day-out basis or when away for a rail tour or special visit. A 1953 visit to Oxford was a family one, so work was more localised, but in 1954 I made the last 'big bash' north of the border.

Unfortunately, domestic affairs enforced the curtailment of darkroom work very suddenly towards the end of 1954. Although photography was continued until 1956, the plates were processed but the enlarging was deferred, except some 'newsy' ones for the journals. Moreover, the shutter blind failed on the press camera, so I left it at that, feeling I had reached the end of an era, even though the end of steam was not forecast until 1970 and I missed the beautiful BR Class 9F 2-10-0s, which I observed but which went unrecorded by the faithful Tessar.

I hope that the viewer will receive as much pleasure in looking through this collection as I had in taking it. Many thanks are, of course, due to the many kind offices shown by the various Regional public relations officers of British Railways, without whose lineside walking photographic permits almost all photographs included would not have been possible.

April 1975

ERIC D. BRUTON
London Colney, Herts

Above: Following a dead stand at signals south of Bushey & Oxhey station, the driver of Stanier 'Black Five' 4-6-0 No 45150 worked the engine really hard in an effort to accelerate to a minimum of 20mph in the short distance from the start to reaching Bushey water troughs, in order to pick up as the locomotive crossed with the up 6.40am Saturday Wolverhampton-Euston express on the cold morning of April 28, 1951. On Mondays to Fridays this train conveyed a restaurant car for the business clientele.

Right: Standard Class 4MT 2-6-4T No 80065 has just left Tring yard on an up pick-up goods train on October 3, 1953 and is travelling on the up slow road.

Above left: The second of the two rebuilt 'Jubilee' Class 4-6-0s, No 5736 *Phoenix* (with double chimney), entering platform No 3 at Euston with the up 11.35pm Glasgow-Euston 'Horse & Cart' (horsebox and carriage wagon train — a description handed down from the early days of trains to carry private carriages on wagons and their horses as well) on April 3, 1948.

Below left: 'Patriot' Class 6P 4-6-0 No 45546 *Fleetwood* in new standard BR lined Brunswick Green livery — quite nicely kept by the home depot of Willesden MPD — is seen near Northchurch on the slow road with the down Saturdays only 1.55pm Euston-Bletchley on March 8, 1952.

Above right: Fowler 'Patriot' Class 4-6-0 No 45510, one of the un-named examples of that class, passing Kings Langley station with the up 8.55am Llandudno and North Wales to London (Euston) express on August 28, 1948

With American bell and commemorative nameplates, including the unusual smokebox nameplate embodying the use of the definite article, Camden-based Fowler 'Royal Scot' Class 4-6-0 No 46100 *Royal Scot,* in BR lined black livery and somewhat work-stained, heads the down 11.25am Euston to Birmingham & Wolverhampton express between Bourne End outer home signals on March 25, 1950.

Right: Fowler 'Patriot' Class 4-6-0 No 45546 *Fleetwood* heads for the short Northchurch Tunnel on a down relief express from Euston to Manchester (London Road), on September 2, 1950, with a very interesting ex-Great Central Railway 'Matchboard' bogie van behind the tender.

Below: My only camera-frame sighting of a Stanier streamlined 'Pacific' and it had to be a unique double-header: tragedy or superb luck? 'Princess Coronation' 4-6-2 No 6226 *Duchess of Norfolk* in dirty (wartime) plain black livery and shortly due for shopping and conversion, is piloted by 'Black Five' 4-6-0 No 5148 on the down, 10.00am Euston to Glasgow (Central) 'Royal Scot' express at Watford Tunnel North signalbox on May 8, 1948.

The last engine of the Stanier 'Jubilee' Class (5XP, later 6P), BR No 45742 *Connaught,* was fitted in 1940 with a double chimney as a prelude to the 1942 rebuilds of No 5735 *Comet* and No 5736 *Phoenix.* The latter pair became the prototypes for the standard rebuilds of both 'Patriot' and 'Royal Scot' class locomotives of 1946 and 1943 respectively. Here *Connaught,* in BR lined Brunswick Green livery, is seen on March 8, 1952 near Northchurch in charge of the down 2.15 pm Euston-Birmingham and Wolverhampton.

Right upper: Aftermath of the Harrow disaster — several services were diverted to St Pancras, one being the up 'Ulster Express'. I went out especially to record this one coming up the Midland Division main line at Radlett on October 11, 1952, headed by rebuilt 'Royal Scot' Class 7P 4-6-0 No 46111 *Royal Fusilier* (in standard Brunswick Green livery).

Right lower: The ex-LMS Royal Train south of Tring, conveying HRH Duke of Edinburgh and HRH Princess Elizabeth on the return from Liverpool (Riverside) at the conclusion of the 1951 Tour of Canada on November 17, 1951. The train is headed by beautifully polished rebuilt 'Royal Scot' 4-6-0 No 46126 *Royal Army Service Corps* of 1B Camden in standard Brunswick Green livery. The burnished buffers mirror the darkness of the shaded track under the bridge just ahead.

Above left: My last plate exposed on a London Midland Region subject was this one of rebuilt 'Royal Scot' Class 4-6-0 No 46139 *The Welch Regiment* climbing Camden Bank, just south of the MPD, with the down 3.20pm Euston-Blackpool (Central) express on July 21, 1955.

Above right: An up Class C parcels and van train heads for Euston at the southern end of Bushey troughs behind G2A Class 7F 0-8-0 No 49099 travelling on the up slow road. June 30 1951

Below right: A push-and-pull working at St Albans Abbey branch terminus. The up 2.45pm train for all stations to Watford Junction is seen on August 14, 1948 being propelled from the station by Stanier Class 2P 0-4-4T No 1908 — one of a small class of ten locomotives introduced in 1932 to replace life-expired locomotives and for which the existing Fowler designs and parts were used.

The prototype BR Class 6MT 'Light Pacific' No 72000 *Clan Buchanan*, still almost 'ex-works' new, pulling away from the Penrith stop with the up 1.45pm Glasgow (Central)–Liverpool (Exchange) express on Thursday May 29, 1952. Note pre-Stanier LMS 12-wheel restaurant car behind the leading brake-composite coach. The obelisk on the 940ft Penrith Beacon is between the tall two-arm signal and the right-hand post of the bracket signal cluster.

The down 1.15 pm 'Midday Scot' did not reach Penrith until evening and here, at 7.01pm, we see Stanier Class 8P 'Princess Coronation' 4-6-2 No 46246 *City of Manchester* swinging the express round the famous Penrith curve on Thursday May 29, 1952, at the limit of 60mph. No 46246 was originally one of the streamlined series, as may be detected from the shaped top of the smokebox (the streamlined casings were removed, commencing in 1946, as locomotives went through Crewe Works for general overhauls). The engine is in blue livery.

Above: Ex-Midland Railway Johnson Class 3F 0-6-0 No 43585 (rebuilt from 1916 by Fowler with a non-superheated Belpaire boiler) was one of the 1885 design. It is in charge of an up West Coast Class K stopping freight near Dillicar troughs, its duties taking it back south towards the home shed of Royston on Monday, May 26, 1952. Tebay village starts in the background, on the A685 Kendal-Kirkby Stephen Road, seen passing the skylined cottage.

Right: Stanier 'Black Five' 4-6-0 No 44907 heads through the Lune Gorge on Dillicar straight on Thursday June 5, 1952 with the up 1.55pm Carlisle-Liverpool (Edge Hill Yard) Class E express freight. Jeffrey's Mount is prominent to the centre of the photograph, with the slopes of Fell Head above the locomotive, to the north of the River Lune.

18

Right: Stanier ex-LMSR Class 5MT 2-6-0 No 42983 is one of a class of only 40 'Moguls' introduced in 1933 with the LMS taper boiler design. It is seen near Shap Wells on Monday May 26, 1952 (with a Fowler tender) and is in charge of the down 7.40am Crewe-Carlisle Class H through freight. Rear-end assistance is provided by Fowler 4MT 2-6-4T No 42403 of Tebay MPD. The Mogul is from Crewe South MPD.

Above left: Viewed from the slopes overlooking Dillicar troughs, in the Lune Valley near Tebay, Stanier Class 8P 'Princess Royal' 4-6-2 No 46203 *Princess Margaret Rose,* in green livery, takes water as it sweeps through at 60mph with the down 11.15am 'Birmingham-Scottish' express from New Street to Glasgow (Central) on Whit Monday June 2, 1952.

Below left: Viewed from the Fells, outside the boundary drystone wall (I was being 'dive-bombed' by angry lapwing — or curlew — I must have been near a nest but did not see it) 'Clan' Class 6MT 4-6-2 No 72001 *Clan Cameron* heads north on Wednesday May 28, 1952, climbing Shap Bank near Scout Green a little way south of the signalbox, with the combined afternoon Scottish express from Manchester and Liverpool. The fourth vehicle is an old LMS 12-wheel dining car in maroon livery.

Below right: The fireman on 'Jubilee' Class 6P 4-6-0 No 45623 *Palestine* has succeeded in obtaining a tender-full on Dillicar troughs with a good overflow to boot, as the engine charges through for a good run at Shap bank with the down 9.55pm Class C Willesden-Carlisle milk tank and parcels train, on Wednesday May 28, 1952.

Above: Carrying the special Oxenholme to Shap Summit piloting turn reporting number 82, Fowler Class 4P 2-6-4T No 42314 from Tebay MPD double-heads Stanier Class 5 4-6-0 No 44708 near Scout Green on the combined 2.00pm Manchester (Victoria) and 2.15pm Liverpool (Exchange) to Glasgow and Edinburgh through express (joining portions at Preston and splitting at Carstairs with some complicated movements). The date was June 9, 1950 and load 15 vehicles.

Left: Fowler (side-window cab type) Class 4MT 2-6-4T No 42404 near Shap Wells pounding away behind the brake-van of the down 11.36am Class FF2 express freight from Garston (Liverpool) on June 9, 1950. A 2¼in square roll film shot.

Ivatt ex-LMS Class 2MT light 2-6-0 No 46471 (a 'Mickey Mouse' to some!) leaving the NE Yard at Tebay on the Fridays only 8.42am Ulverston-Durham 'miners' special, June 6, 1952. It will travel via Kirkby Stephen (East), 'Stainmore Summit,' Barnard Castle and Bishop Auckland. Note interesting assortment of vintage vehicles. Loups Fell dominates the whole background.

Above left: Barrow MPD-based, Fowler Class 4F 0-6-0 No 44487 is working home through the Lune Gorge, at Dillicar, with the up 9.42am Class J Tebay to Lindal coke train on Wednesday May 28, 1952. The coke wagons have previously been brought from the north-eastern coke oven plants via Stainmore Summit and Kirkby Stephen to Tebay Yard, for transfer to LMR.

Below left: The down 10.00am 'Royal Scot', nearly two hours late due to Sunday engineering diversions further south, swings from Dillicar straight into the winding section towards Dillicar troughs and Tebay as it rushes for Shap Bank at a mile a minute on May 25, 1952. The side-on evening sun (5.15pm) illuminates the wheels and motion of Stanier Class 8P 'Princess Coronation' 4-6-2 No 46236 *City of Bradford* (in the BR Caledonian Blue livery of those years) to perfection.

Right: Webb ex-LNWR 18in goods 'Cauliflower' 0-6-0 goods engine (1887 design) BR No 58389, shunting at Penrith goods yard on June 15, 1950 with Penrith Beacon in the background.

Above: Class G2A 0-8-0 No 49027 (a 1936 rebuild of Bowen-Cooke's Class G1 design, fitted with a type G2 Belpaire boiler). The locomotive is seen heading an up Class E freight through Penrith on Thursday May 29, 1952.

Above: With the village of Tebay in the background and the Station Hotel prominent above the second vehicle, gleaming Stanier 'Jubilee' Class 4-6-0 No 45706 *Express* in standard Brunswick Green livery rushes Shap Bank, scorning a banker with the 13-coach load. The train is the down 4.25pm Liverpool (Exchange)-Glasgow (Central) on the beautiful evening of Tuesday June 3, 1952. The 'Jubilee', paired with a Fowler standard 3,500 gal tender, is a Newton Heath MPD engine, probably on a triangular working.

Below: This is limestone country and the familiar rounded profile of Fell Head dominates the skyline at Dillicar Straight, with the still infant River Lune on the left. BR 'Clan' Class 4-6-2 No 72001 *Clan Cameron* storms northwards with the combined afternoon Manchester and Liverpool 'Scottish Express' on Thursday June 5, 1952.

Above: The 10.35am Tebay to Kirkby Stephen one-coach conductor guard-operated (yes-even then!) branch train, shortly after leaving the NE platform at Tebay station. It is headed by a 'Mickey Mouse', i.e., Ivatt Class 2MT 2-6-0 No 46480 from 51A Darlington MPD. Friday, May 30, 1952.

Left: The down 4.10pm Oxenholme-Windermere branch train near Oxenholme on June 4, 1952 headed by Stanier two-cylinder Class 4MT 2-6-4T No 42573.

Right: Carnforth MPD's very smartly turned-out Stanier two-cylinder, taper-boiler Class 4MT 2-6-4T No 42601, passing Dillicar troughs on the up 1.51pm Carlisle-Oxenholme stopping train, a filling-in turn for Newcastle-Carlisle sets, hence the ex-LNER stock. Tebay railwaymen referred to these locals as the 'Little Aberdeens' to distinguish them from the Euston-Carlisle expresses, locally known as the 'Big Aberdeens'. Whit-Monday afternoon June 2, 1952.

Below: The up 3.12pm Workington Main-Liverpool (Exchange) stopping train leaving Ravenglass on September 4, 1954. Fowler Class 4MT two-cylinder 2-6-4T No 42401 (one of the series introduced in 1933 with side-window cabs) is piloted by Stanier two-cylinder Class 4MT 2-6-4T No 42427 (introduced in 1935).

Above: BR 'Clan' Class 4-6-2 No 72001 *Clan Cameron* nearing the final pair of rock cuttings into Shap Fell on Monday May 26, 1952. It is making about 30mph with the combined 2.00pm Manchester (Victoria) and 2.15pm Liverpool (Exchange) restaurant car express to Glasgow and Edinburgh, the 13 vehicles of which are a mixture of maroon and carmine and cream livery.

Below: From out on the fell 'Patriot' (Class 6P) 4-6-0 No 45549 is seen near Birdcage Bridge cutting at Shap Wells with the down 10.40am Crewe-Carlisle Class D express freight, assisted in the rear by Fowler Class 4MT 2-6-4T No 42396 on Friday June 6, 1952.

Above right: With the high fells flanking the winding Lune Gorge between Dillicar Straight and the water troughs nearer to Tebay, Stanier 'Jubilee' Class 6P 4-6-0 No 45695 *Minotaur,* with a nicely polished boiler and firebox, charges through the reverse curves for Shap Bank with the down 9.30am Liverpool (Exchange)-Glasgow (Central) express on Monday May 26, 1952.

Below right: Sunday afternoon empty ballast train, headed by ex-LNWR 0-8-0 No 49396, at Dillicar on May 25, 1952.

Above left: Stanier ex-LMS Class 7P 'Princess Coronation' 4-6-2 No 46222 *Queen Mary,* originally one of the streamlined series until 'defrocked'. It is passing Penrith on June 15, 1950 with the up 'Royal Scot' express having observed the permanent 60mph speed order through the Penrith curve in the background.

Below left: My first sighting of a BR 'Clan' Pacific. Class 6MT 4-6-2 No 72004 *Clan Macdonald* (almost brand new) was caught storming away from the Lancaster stop and passing the magnificent LNWR two-storey brick built Lancaster No 4 signal box with the down 9.43am Liverpool (Exchange)-Glasgow (Central) express at 11.10am on Saturday, May 24, 1952. All eleven coaches are finished in standard carmine and cream livery.

Above left: Usually a Pacific turn, in spite of its relatively humble secondary express nature, the down 10.40am Euston-Carlisle is seen on Wednesday May 28, 1952 passing Scout Green signal box — about midway up the 1 in 75 gradient from Tebay North to Shap Summit. Motive power is Stanier 'de-frocked' 4-6-2 No 46228 *Duchess of Rutland* in BR's experimental lined-blue livery and quite smartly turned out by the cleaners at the home 'shed' of Carlisle (Upperby).

Below left: Stanier 8P 'Princess Royal' Class 4-6-2 No 46203 *Princess Margaret Rose,* in standard BR green livery, heads past that well-known gangers' hut at Shap Wells on Friday June 6 1952 with the down 11.15am 'Birmingham-Scottish' express. Speed is down to about 20mph but there is not far to climb now.

Above right: A 'Black Five' north of the border, in former LNER (NBR) territory. Here No 45488 from Perth MPD (63A) is seen storming through Haymarket station, Edinburgh, heading the down 6.55pm express from Waverley station to Perth (via the Forth Bridge and Glenfarg) on June 8, 1951.

Below right: On June 9, 1948 Stanier 2-6-0 No 2948 wheels the up 2.45pm Bangor-Llandudno Junction stopping train from the darkness of the up line tube of Robert Stephenson's twin-tubed Conway Bridge.

Above: 'Royal Scot' Class (Fowler) 4-6-0 No 6113 *Cameronian* passing Colwyn Bay on the five-coach up second portion of the 'Irish Mail' on June 5, 1948.

Below: The 7.05am Plymouth-Liverpool express (via the Severn Tunnel and Hereford) swinging away from Shrewsbury station round the sharp curve to the Crewe line is headed by 'Patriot' Class 4-6-0 No 45538 *Giggleswick* in BR green livery, on Sunday April 27, 1952.

Above: Fowler 1924 LMSR series standard compound three-cylinder Class 4P 4-4-0 No 1118 passing the golf course at Maes Du, between Deganwy and Llandudno, with the 4.15pm Liverpool (Lime Street) — Llandudno express on June 8, 1948. The engine is in LMS post-war unlined black livery, but quite clean. Coaches, all in LMS maroon, are 'Blackpool residential set No 2', presumably on a filling-in turn.

Below: 'Patriot' class 4-6-0 No 45537 *Private E. Sykes VC* in new BR dark green livery near Clifton with the up 4.20pm Sunday Carlisle-Manchester (Victoria) Class B stopping train on June 11, 1950. The engine is from Preston MPD.

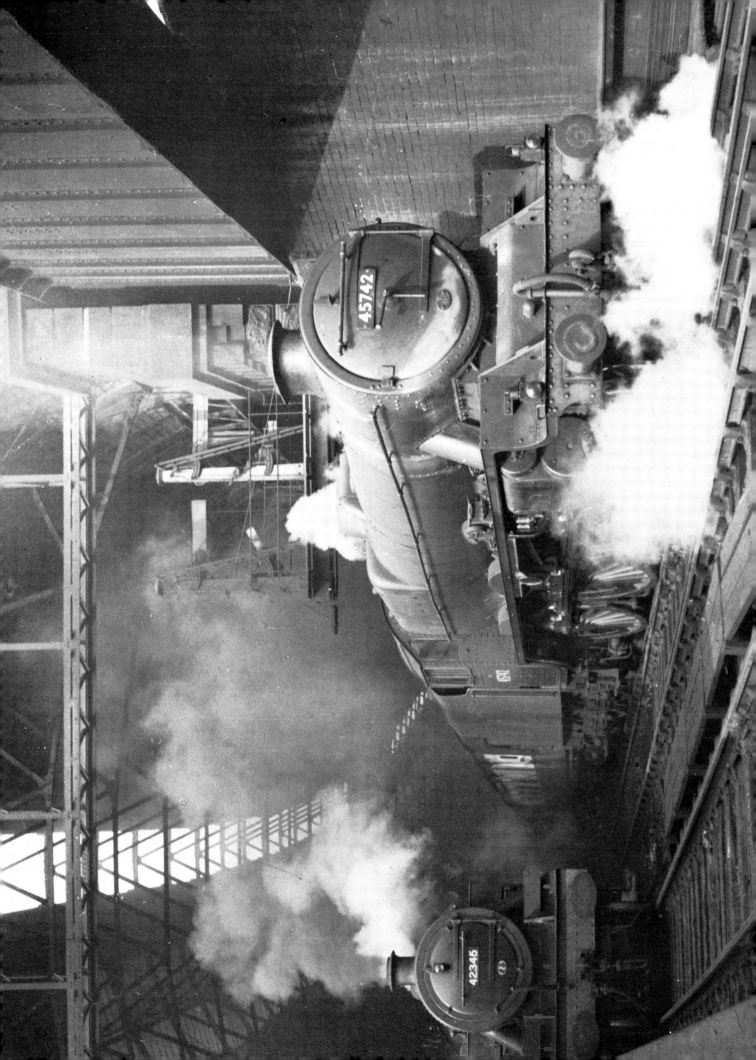

Above: The Birmingham (New Street) station scene on Sunday September 13, 1953, showing the up 10.30am Wolverhampton-Euston express, headed by double-chimney 'Jubilee' 4-6-0 No 45742 *Connaught*, just starting to move under the authority of the calling-on arm. Fowler Class 4MT 2-6-4T No 42345 — one of the first series introduced to the LMS in 1927 — waits at the opposite platform with a stopping train to Coventry (a 2¼in square roll film shot).

Below: Class 4P compound 4-4-0 No 41038 passing Napsbury on up special No M 768. The engine, from Bedford MPD, is paired with a standard Fowler tender without coal rails.

Above left: Nicknamed 'Bandies', the Caprotti valve gear Stanier 'Black Five' 4-6-0s were certainly unique in appearance amongst British steam locomotives. Here, a Bristol (Barrow Road) MPD-based example of the Class, No 44743, is seen rumbling past Sheffield South No 1 box with the northbound 2,12 pm Bristol-York express, slowing for the stop at Sheffield (Midland) station on May 10, 1952.

Below left: The SLS/MLS 'Hull & Barnsley Rail Tour' special, originating from Manchester (Central) and travelling to Hull via the Hull & Barnsley route, has paused at Sheffield (Midland) on August 24, 1952. Ex-Midland Railway Johnson (rebuilt) Class 3P 4-4-0 No 40726 from Canklow MPD has worked from Manchester via Chinley and will be replaced at Cudworth by an ex-NER Class D20/2 for the journey over the H&B metals. At the island platform face, a down stopping train waits for time and the road, headed by ex-LMS (1924 series) Fowler 6ft 9in three-cylinder compound 4-4-0 No 40910. This series outlived the Deeley ex-Midland Railway compounds, Nos 1000-1044, which had gone by the end of 1954 — as indeed had those handsome 3P 4-4-0s.

Above right: The up 9.20am 'Thames-Clyde Express' from Glasgow (St Enoch) passing Dore & Totley South junction in the charge of Stanier 'Jubilee' Class 4-6-0 No 45573 *Newfoundland,* which is accelerating away towards Bradway Tunnel, although still climbing at 1 in 100 until the south portal is reached. Saturday June 19, 1954.

Above: An unusual double-heading as the up 7.10am Sheffield-St. Pancras express heads through Harper Lane cutting, north of Radlett, on April 30, 1949 with Horwich-built Hughes/Fowler 'Crab' 2-6-0 No 42846 piloting Stanier 'Jubilee' Class 4-6-0 No 45656 *Cochrane.* Note that the tender of the 'Crab' is still plainly lettered LMS and that these initials have been lovingly cleaned!

Below: On May 7, 1949 Horwich 'Crab' 2-6-0 No 42763, quite clean and with LMS on the tender, pilots ex-LMS Fowler/Beyer Peacock 2-6-6-2T Beyer-Garratt No 47987 on a down empty mineral wagon train, on the straight stretch of quadruple track to Harpenden Arches.

Below: An unusual combination is seen in this Bromsgrove shot on April 16, 1955 as the Fowler ex-Midland Railway 0-10-0 Lickey Incline banking engine No 58100 (introduced in 1919) buffers up to the ex-LNER beaver-tail observation car, from the erstwhile 'Coronation' express. This coach was in use that day on a *Trains Illustrated* special train, 'The Lickey Limited.'

Above: Ivatt Class 4MT light 2-6-0 No 43010 — a type nicknamed 'Flying Pigs' by many enthusiasts — is piloting Stanier 'Black Five' 4-6-0 No 44822 near Radlett on a down Class C express goods, probably from Somers Town goods depot and yard, on July 14, 1951.

Left: Carrying the special three-headlamp code denoting a through train to and from Moorgate, Fowler ex-LMS Class 3MT 2-6-2T No 40039 (a condensing locomotive introduced in 1930 for the Moorgate service) heads the down 5.56pm Moorgate-St Albans all stations stopping train up the 1 in 176 gradient north of Radlett at 6.53pm on July 24, 1950.

Below left: Ex-Midland Railway Johnson Class 2F 0-6-0 No 58235 (ex-LMS No 3150) was one of the design introduced in 1875 and subsequently rebuilt with a Belpaire boiler (non-superheated). The locomotive is seen about to pass under Harper Lane Bridge, north of Radlett, with an up Luton-Cricklewood pick-up goods on June 26, 1948.

Below right: BR Standard Class 5MT 4-6-0 locomotives Nos 73000 (train engine) and 73001 (pilot) head one of the Derby research team's special vacuum-fitted express coal train trials, with dynamometer car in use, near Harpenden Common at a controlled 40mph on October 26, 1952.

Above: Experimental apple green livery adorns Class 5XP 'Jubilee' 4-6-0 No 45694 *Bellerophon* with the interim British Railways lettering on the tender, as it starts very gently away from St Pancras station heading the down 4.50pm Bradford (Forster Square) express comprising stock in cream and brown livery — virtually GWR coach colours. A pretty sight!

Below: The down 4.30pm St Pancras-Nottingham train leaving St Pancras on August 25, 1948 against the familiar 'backdrop' of the gasholders and the rather unique double hip-roofed ex-Midland signalbox. Blowing a bit at the nearside gland, Stanier 'Jubilee' class 5XP 4-6-0 No 45648 *Wemyss,* in black livery with lining-out only on cab and tender, heads the train.

Above: Fowler/Beyer Peacock (1930 type) Beyer-Garratt 2-6-6-2T No 47995 passing Chiltern Green, south of Luton, on an up Toton-Cricklewood mixed goods and mineral wagon train on July 28, 1951. The rotary bunker of this series is just visible behind the upper half of the cab.

Below: One of the then 26 remaining locomotives of Johnson's Class 3P 4-4-0 (6ft 9in) Midland Railway 1921 rebuilds, No 762, is seen accelerating southwards from the St Albans stop on the up fast line, as it clears Napsbury Lane Bridge with the up 9.07am Bedford-St Pancras semi-fast. Note the ex-MR signal (Napsbury advanced starter) covering the down slow road, April 24, 1948.

Above left: An up Toton-Cricklewood Class J block coal train heads down the 1 in 176 gradient at Harper Lane Bridge, between Napsbury and Radlett, on April 30, 1949; it is headed by wartime-built (Southern Railway-Brighton Works) Stanier Class 8F 2-8-0 No 48692. The engine is from Sheffield MPD and has automatic 'blowdown' gear fitted, hence the warning 'X' painted each side on the lower cabside sheet.

Below left: Deeley ex-Midland Railway three-cylinder compound 7ft 0in 4-4-0 No 1044 is the last locomotive of a class of 45 introduced in 1905, numbered 1000-1044 and subsequently superheated by Fowler. Fortunately No 1000 of this series is preserved. No 1044 is on the 1 in 176 gradient climbing towards St Albans with the down 6.52pm St Pancras-Bedford semi-fast on Friday August 4, 1950.

Above: Green-liveried Stanier 'Jubilee' 4-6-0 No 45607 *Fiji* seen north of Sandridge summit, between St Albans and Harpenden, accelerating the down 6.40pm St Pancras-Sheffield away from the summit of the 1 in 176 climb from the Colne Viaduct near Radlett on July 19, 1951.

Left: A Hughes-Fowler Horwich-built 2-6-0 of 1926 LMS design and Class 5F but universally known as 'Horwich Crabs' — No 42874 of Rowsley shed and, externally at any rate, quite a credit to them for a mixed traffic locomotive — heads north along the LMS Midland Division main line at Napsbury station, on the 1 in 176 bank through to Sandridge Summit, with an evening non-fitted express Class F goods from Cricklewood to Derby on July 21, 1950.

Below: BR standard 'Clan' class light Pacific No 72009 *Clan Stewart* heads northwards with the down 11.50am stopping train from Hellifield to Carlisle, out on the open fell near Smardale. Note the non-corridor coach at the tail of the train in plain BR suburban red livery.

Right. An ex-Midland Railway Johnson Class 2P 7ft 0½in 4-4-0, BR No 40502, was one of a series built between 1891 and 1901 but subsequently rebuilt by Fowler from 1912 with superheaters and piston valves. The locomotive, from Hasland MPD, is seen leaving Dore & Totley station with the up 12.20pm Sheffield (Midland) to Chesterfield stopping train on Saturday June 19, 1954.

Below: Stanier 'Black Fives' in tandem, a common enough sight on the Settle-Carlisle 'Long Drag' in either direction. Nos 44878 and 44775 are seen leaving Smardale Viaduct on the up 10.03am Edinburgh (Waverley) to Leeds and St Pancras express on Tuesday June 3, 1952.

Above: Gresley Class A4 4-6-2 No 60033 *Seagull*, with Kylchap blastpipe and double chimney, picking up water on Langley troughs, near Stevenage, at the head of an up express for Kings Cross on November 3, 1951. The Kings Cross A4 is in dark blue livery.

Below: The down 7.00pm 'Aberdonian' sleeping car express from Kings Cross to Edinburgh (Waverley) and Aberdeen also carried through sleepers for Fort William via Glasgow (Queen Street). The motive power on the evening of August 2, 1951 was Gresley Class V2 2-6-2 No 60938, from New England MPD, Peterborough. It is seen emerging from Hadley North tunnel.

Above: The heavy 3.30pm Kings Cross-Newcastle express near Marshmoor on April 15, 1950 headed by Gresley Class A3 4-6-2 No 60110 *Robert the Devil,* with interim British Railways lettering on the tender.

Below: Gresley Class A3 4-6-2 No 60039 *Sandwich* heads the down 10.00am Kings Cross-Edinburgh (Waverley) 'Scotsman' north towards Hatfield, near Red Hall signalbox, on the cloudless morning of April 16, 1949. The locomotive is in the post-war LNER apple green livery with limited lining and British Railways ownership.

Above: In gleaming BR experimental blue livery, contrasting nicely with the Pullman Car Company colours of the stock, Peppercorn Class A1 4-6-2 No 60117 *Bois Roussel* maintains 60mph with some steam on down the bank from Potters Bar tunnel at Ganwick with the up 10.17am Harrogate-Kings Cross 'Yorkshire Pullman' on March 20, 1951.

Below: The up 10.15am Leeds & Harrogate express south of Brookmans Park on April 9, 1949, headed by Gresley Class A3 4-6-2 No 60103 *Flying Scotsman,* now privately preserved under its old number of LNER 4472.

Above: Class N2/2 condensing 0-6-2T No 69493 about to blast into Hadley Wood North tunnel with the down (Sunday) 1.59pm Kings Cross-Hatfield 'stopper' on March 4, 1951 after the Hadley Wood stop.

Right: Hitchin MPD provided this reasonably clean Thompson Class L1 2-6-4T No 67743, which is seen between the tunnels at Ganwick on the evening of August 2, 1951. It heads a down outer suburban train from Kings Cross.

Right: Local trains were usually spectacular in the way in which they were worked hard between frequent stops. This one, the down 2.59pm Kings Cross stopping train, is no exception. With the train just clear of Hadley Wood North tunnel and accelerating away from the Hadley Wood station stop, the exhaust of Gresley Class N2/2 0-6-2T (condensing) locomotive No 69521 forms a nicely billowing pattern of smoke and steam in the light cross wind of the afternoon of March 20, 1951.

Above right: On August holiday weekend, 1951, a relief 'Aberdonian' was hauled by Class A4 4-6-2 No 60010 *Dominion of Canada* in dark blue livery. It is emerging from Hadley Wood North tunnel. No 60010 carries the Canadian Pacific Railways presentation bell, fitted in March, 1938; this was steam-operated with Bowden cable control but was rendered inoperative in pre-war days following a failure. In the photograph the engine carries a standard chime whistle, but between May 1937 and April 1949 it carried a CPR chime whistle.

Above left: Another beautifully polished locomotive, Copley Hill MPD-based, green-liveried Class A1 4-6-2 No 60120 *Kittiwake* is seen picking up water on Langley troughs, heading the up 'Yorkshire Pullman' express from Leeds (Central) on November 3, 1951.

Below left: The 'Northern Rubber Special 1871-1951' with circular headboard depicting the founder of the company, ran up the ex-GNR main line from Retford on Saturday September 8, 1951 with a works outing party, headed by Thompson Class A1/1 4-6-2 No 60113 *Great Northern* in blue livery; the special is seen at Ganwick.

Above right: Gresley Class K3/2 2-6-0 No 61954 from New England MPD, Peterborough, passing Langley troughs with an up Class K stopping mixed freight train on May 12, 1951. Note the clerestory-roofed van on the adjacent siding. This is a weighing machine tool and maintenance van, no doubt the weighbridge in the yard was receiving attention.

Below right: Ex-LNER Class J20/1 0-6-0 No 64678 was a rebuild of the Hill GER design introduced in 1920 with an LNER B12/1 round-topped boiler. No 64678 is dropping down the 1 in 200 gradient at Ganwick, heading an up Class F non-fitted through express freight from the depths of Potters Bar tunnel on March 20, 1951. The engine was based in the Immingham/Lincoln/Boston area, as Code 40 is just discernible with an eyeglass.

Below left: Gresley ex-LNER Class V2 2-6-2 No 60911 storms the bank at Ganwick, hurrying a down afternoon Class C express freight from London out of the depths of Hadley Wood North tunnel, on March 20, 1951.

Above left: Double-headers at the London end of the ex-GNR main line were rare indeed, usually indicating some trouble. Gresley Class A3 4-6-2 No 60108 *Gay Crusader,* not feeling so gay on July 7, 1951, had failed at Knebworth and took the assistance of Class B1 4-6-0 No 61113 to carry on to Kings Cross with the up 8.25am (Saturdays only) Newcastle express, recorded at Greenwood up splitting signals.

Below left: Gresley Class W1 streamlined 4-6-4 No 60700 drifts down the 1 in 200 gradient at Ganwick on an unidentified up parcels or pigeon van train heading for the Hadley tunnels and Kings Cross on September 8, 1951. No 60700 was the Gresley 1937 rebuild of his former LNER 'Hush-Hush' 4-6-4 No 10000 of 1929. The engine is in nicely-kept BR experimental dark blue livery.

Above right: The morning Class D down express fish vans train from Maiden Lane (Kings Cross) heading north from Hadley Wood North tunnel on the slightly frosty morning of April 14, 1951. Gresley Class K3/2 2-6-0 No 61868 is blasting up the 1 in 200 gradient at about 30mph.

Above left: Gresley Class B17/4 4-6-0 No 61655 *Middlesbrough* was in BR Brunswick Green livery when photographed on May 12, 1951 picking up water on Langley troughs, south of Stevenage, in charge of an up secondary express for Kings Cross.

Below left: My last plate before the shutter 'went for a Burton' was this one on March 10, 1956. It depicts Class A4 4-6-2 No 60006 *Sir Ralph Wedgwood* on a Leeds-Kings Cross express just north of Stevenage.

Above right: The down 10.18am Kings Cross-Leeds & Bradford express, headed by Gresley Class A4 4-6-2 No 60014 *Silver Link* about to plunge into Hadley South tunnel on April 14, 1952.

Above left: Trailing a Thompson slab-sided toplight full brake, Class A1 4-6-2 No 60149 *Amadis* bursts from Hadley Wood North tunnel with the down 9.18am 'White Rose' express from Kings Cross to Leeds (Central) on September 8, 1951.

Below left: The up 1.50pm Cambridge-Kings Cross semi-fast dropping down the 1 in 200 gradient through Hadley Wood station headed by Cambridge MPD-based green-liveried Class B17/6 4-6-0 No 61627 *Aske Hall* on March 4, 1951.

Above right: Shedding the last of a heavy overfill on Langley troughs, Gresley Class B17/4 4-6-0 No 61652 *Darlington* in standard BR green livery heads a down semi-fast train from Kings Cross, on November 3, 1951.

Above left: The down 9.30am 'Capitals Limited' express from Kings Cross to Edinburgh (Waverley) leaving Hadley North tunnel at Ganwick headed by Class A4 4-6-2 No 60025 *Falcon* in BR blue livery on September 8, 1951.

Above right: Passing the Marshmoor repeater signals, Class V2 2-6-2 No 60935 heads for Kings Cross with an up express from Harrogate on April 15, 1950.

Below right: Complete with its transatlantic bell, Gresley Class A4 4-6-2 No 60010 *Dominion of Canada* in BR standard Brunswick Green livery clears the GNR overbridge at Marshmoor, south of Hatfield, with the down 4.45pm 'Tees-Tyne Pullman' express from London, Kings Cross, on September 14, 1953.

Above: Thompson two-cylinder Class B2 4-6-0 No 61632 *Belvoir Castle* (a 1945 rebuild from the three-cylinder Gresley B17 'Sandringham' locomotive), blasts up Brentwood bank with a buffet car express from Liverpool Street to East Anglia on March 24, 1951.

Above: 'Britannia' class 4-6-2 locomotive No 70001
Lord Hurcomb climbing the 1 in 85/155 gradient of
Brentwood Bank with the down 10.00am 'The
Norfolkman' Liverpool Street—Norwich (Thorpe)
express on March 24, 1951.

Right: The Liverpool Street station pilot, ex-GER Class
J69 0-6-0T No E8619, resplendent in BR apple green
livery and highly polished, waits on the sidings
between platforms 9 and 10 with a rake of assorted
wagons.

Above left: On the ex-GCR, Thompson Class B1 4-6-0 No 61248 *Geoffrey Gibbs* from Doncaster MPD is leaving Sheffield Victoria with the up 2.56pm Sheffield-Doncaster stopping train on May 10, 1952.

Below left: Worsdell ex-NER Class J25 0-6-0 No 65695 from Kirkby Stephen MPD heading a 25-wagon mixed freight and coke train westwards near Gaisgill (Kirkby Stephen to Tebay line) under the Class J headlamp code on Friday, May 30 1952.

Below right: The Mound tunnel separates the West Princes Street Gardens cutting from the shorter East Princes Street Gardens cutting, Waverley bridge and Waverley station, Edinburgh. It also passes directly under the Mound Road and the National Portrait Gallery of Scotland. In this photograph Thompson Class A2/1 4-6-2 No 60507 *Highland Chieftain* is threading the tunnel with the 2.15pm Edinburgh-Aberdeen on June 22, 1954.

Above left: Familiar brickwork to RAF types who 'square-bashed' in the nearby camp, for the station is Padgate, CLC lines, near Warrington. Passing through is Heaton Mersey MPD-based Robinson ex-GCR 'Large Director' Class D11/1 4-4-0 No 62663 *Prince Albert* on a down Class H through freight for the Manchester area on Saturday October 17, 1953.

Below left: 'Austerity' 2-8-0 No 90513, stationed at Dunfermline MPD, storms the 1 in 70 gradient of the Inverkeithing-North Queensferry Bank with an up Class H through freight. Rear-end assistance is provided by the Inverkeithing banker, ex-NBR Class J35/4 0-6-0 No 64513, Tuesday, June 29, 1954.

Above right: On the dull morning of Thursday July 1, 1954 the up 9.45am 'Elizabethan' Edinburgh (Waverley)-Kings Cross express is clearing Calton Hill main line tunnel, Edinburgh, headed by gleaming Kings Cross Class A4 4-6-2 No 60030 *Golden Fleece.*

The 11.00am Glasgow (Queen Street)-Kings Cross 'Queen of Scots' Pullman express approaching Grantshouse at the end of the long climb of Cockburnspath bank, but still doing 50mph or better in the charge of Gresley Class A3 4-6-2 No 60043 *Brown Jack* from Haymarket MPD. Not long afterward rain swept over from the West to upset most of the day's lineside activities on Saturday, June 26 1954.

Above: A nicely polished, Brunswick Green-liveried engine from Dundee (Tay Bridge) MPD is Peppercorn Class A2 4-6-2 No 60527 *Sun Chariot.* The locomotive is seen on the 1 in 70 gradient of the North Queensferry Bank, approaching North Queensferry tunnel in charge of an up Class C express fish train from Aberdeen on June 8, 1951

Below right: Ex-NBR 'Glen' Class 4-4-0 No 62490 *Glen Fintaig,* LNER Class D34, is seen on Saturday June 26, 1954 heading a Class J mineral and empty wagon train from the Edinburgh area up the last bit of Cockburnspath Bank en route for the sidings at Grantshouse station. 62490 is from St Margarets MPD Edinburgh. It is in BR lined black livery, rather work-stained.

Haymarket MPD, Edinburgh, has provided this beautifully turned-out Gresley Class A3 4-6-2 No 60037 *Hyperion* in the experimental dark blue livery sometimes termed Caledonian Blue. It is seen leaving Waverley station, Edinburgh, in charge of the up 11.00am Glasgow (Queen Street) — Kings Cross 'Queen of Scots' Pullman express on June 8, 1951. This is a 2¼in sq roll film shot.

Above: The rain is getting nearer and direct sunlight has gone but the light is still good enough as Gresley A4 Class 4-6-2 No 60002 *Sir Murrough Wilson,* paired with a non-corridor tender (and both rather 'grubby'), swings round the curve leading from Penmanshiel tunnel near the summit of the 1 in 96/200 Cockburnspath Bank, about one mile north of Grantshouse station. It is making about 40mph with an up relief express from Edinburgh (Waverley) on Saturday, June 26 1954.

Above: Gresley Class A3 4-6-2 No 60057 *Ormonde* storms North Queensferry Bank on Tuesday June 29, 1954 with the up 12.40pm Aberdeen to Edinburgh express. At the time No 60057 was shedded at Haymarket MPD and was in BR Brunswick Green livery.

Right: Gresley Class D49/1 4-4-0 No 62702 *Oxfordshire* threads West Princes Street Gardens, Edinburgh, with the 10.50am Waverley-Thornton Junction stopping train on June 9, 1951.

Above: Gresley Class V3 2-6-2T No 67606 storms through North Queensferry with an up fast on June 8, 1951 at 5.28pm.

Left: Photographed from Forth Bridge North signalbox, a St Margarets MPD-based Gresley Class J38 0-6-0 No 65929, one of a series introduced in 1926, heads a Niddrie Yard-Perth Class D express goods train over the last few yards of the Forth Bridge on June 8, 1951.

Above: Class D11/2 4-4-0 No 62681 *Captain Craigengelt* is slogging up the last hundred yards of the 1 in 70 gradient of the North Queensferry Bank to the summit tunnel, heading the 10.56am Thornton Junction — Edinburgh (Waverley) on Tuesday, June 29 1954.

Right: The up 11.00am 'Queen of Scots' Pullman express from Glasgow (Queen Street) is getting into its stride after the Edinburgh (Waverley) stop, as it swings away from the Waverley route lines at Portobello East Junction, headed by Peppercorn Class A2 4-6-2 No 60537 *Bachelor's Button,* on Wednesday, June 23, 1954.

Above left: Just topping the 1 in 96 portion of Cockburnspath Bank and clear of Penmanshiel tunnel, after about 4½ miles of hard slogging on the curving incline, Class B1 4-6-0 No 61398 makes about 30mph with the up 3.45pm Edinburgh (Waverley)-Berwick stopping train on Saturday June 26, 1954.

Below left: An up train of empty coaching stock, strangely travelling under Class F express non-fitted freight headcode instead of the usual Class C for such trains, is seen on the 1 in 59 gradient about 2½ miles from Fort William, on the West Highland main line, headed by Gresley Class K2/2 2-6-0 No 61786 on Saturday, June 16, 1951.

Below: With snow still lying in the corries of the 4,406ft-high Ben Nevis, which dominates the background, Gresley Class K2/2 2-6-0 No 61789 *Loch Laidon* has shut off steam for the permanent slack over the Caledonian Canal at Banavie swing bridge. The Fort William-based locomotive heads the afternoon Class C empty fish vans from Glenlochy sidings (Mallaig Junction) to Mallaig on Saturday, June 16 1951. Note the vintage North British Railway lattice-post signal with the 'pagoda-topped lamp and without a ladder. The lamp was winch operated.

Above: The down 4.50pm Fort William-Mallaig comprising four bogie corridors in immaculate carmine and cream livery at Banavie, headed by Gresley Class K4 2-6-0 No 61995 *Cameron of Lochiel* in post-war LNER green livery on June 16, 1951

Below: The 9.29am Fort William-Glasgow (Queen Street) leaving the typical NBR island platform station of Cranlarich (Upper) on June 23, 1951 at noon. The usual West Highland double-heading is by Eastfield MPD-based Gresley K2/2 2-6-0 No 61769 piloting sister locomotive No 61774 *Loch Garry.*

Above: Beautifully illuminated by the evening sunshine, Collett '6800' Class 4-6-0 No 6813 *Estbury Grange* (built in 1936) leans to the curving causeway across Cockwood Harbour as it heads up the Exe estuary, accelerating the weekday 5.30pm stopping train from Kingswear to Exeter (St Davids) away from the Starcross stop on Wednesday June 8, 1949.

Below: Churchward 'Star' class 4-6-0 No 4043 *Prince Henry,* built in May, 1913, is seen near Dawlish Warren heading the northbound 10.00am Sunday Paignton-Newcastle express, comprising ex-LNER stock, on Whit-Sunday June 5, 1949.

Above left: The up 10.20am Paignton & Torquay-Paddington Saturdays only express ran non-stop from Torquay to the terminus. Saturday June 4, 1949 sees this train just east of Dawlish, under the red sandstone cliffs, headed by 'King' Class 4-6-0 No 6015 *King Richard III.*

Above right: Riddles ex-Ministry of Supply (War Department) 2-8-0 No 77388 was purchased by BR in 1948 along with the whole class as released by the WD. Classified 8F for power, the series was later renumbered 90000-90732. No 77388 is seen near Parsons Tunnel signalbox on the Teignmouth sea wall section, in charge of a Class C up potato special express freight on Thursday, June 2, 1949.

Below left: In pouring rain, 'Star' Class 4-6-0 No 4056 *Princess Margaret* waits at Exeter (St Davids) station with the RCTS 25th Anniversary special train for the return journey to London (Waterloo) on Sunday, June 28 1953.

Above: Almost a 'Star'. No 4000 *North Star* was unique amongst the 'Castle' class 4-6-0 locomotives. In November, 1929, it was rebuilt from a 'Star' which in turn had been converted in November, 1909 by Churchward from a 4-4-2 locomotive built in April, 1906. It is seen on Monday, May 30 1949 on the Teignmouth sea wall heading the up 9.00am Paignton-Manchester (Mayfield) express via Bristol and the Severn Tunnel.

Left: Hawksworth 'County' class 4-6-0 No 1012 *County of Denbigh*, built in 1946, leaving the Teignmouth end of Parson's Tunnel with the down 5.30am 'newspaper' — the early morning Paddington-Penzance semi fast via Swindon, Bath and Bristol.

Above right: The 11.25am Kingswear-Paddington 'Torbay Express' ran non-stop from Torquay to Exeter, St Davids, on weekdays then non-stop to Paddington. On Saturdays the Exeter stop was omitted. The photograph depicts the Wednesday train on June 1, 1949 headed by 'Castle' class 4-6-0 No 4086 *Builth Castle* on the severely restricted curving section by the 'Salty' at Teighmouth.

Above left: '4073' Class 4-6-0 No 7000 *Viscount Portal* built in May, 1946 with three-row superheater and, when photographed, paired with a Hawksworth slab-sided 4,000 gallon tender, as originally introduced for the 'County' class 4-6-0s. No 7000 is just east of 'Splash Point' on the Teignmouth sea wall in charge of the up 8.45am Plymouth-Liverpool & Manchester express on Friday, June 10 1949.

Below left: The 10.30am 'Cornish Riviera Express' from Paddington, with a rake of carmine and cream stock, heads past the 'Salty' at Teignmouth with blue-liveried 'King' No 6027 *King Richard I* in charge on June 10, 1949.

Above: The up 8.30am Plymouth-Paddington express, generally known as the up 'Dutchman' although not officially named, leans into the curve from station to sea wall at Teignmouth, South Devon. The express is headed by 'King' Class 4-6-0 No 6024 *King Edward I* on May 30, 1949.

Below: Not far from Parsons Tunnel signalbox Churchward '2800 class 2-8-0 No 2861 — one of the orignal series introduced in 1903 and subsequently fitted with a new, superheated boiler — in almost ex-works condition, heads east on May 30, 1949 with an up Class J empty mineral wagon train, which mainly comprises seven-plank wooden coal wagons.

Above right: At 1.30pm on Friday June 10, 1949 the up 9.45am Penzance-Paddington 'Cornish Riviera Express' passes the 'Salty' at Teignmouth. Hauling a rake of newly painted carmine and cream stock is 'King' Class 4-6-0 No 6025 *King Henry III* in experimental blue livery and with 'British Railways' on the tender.

Below left: Churchward '5300' class 2-6-0 No 6393 built in 1921 leaves Parsons Tunnel with a down class C express fish vans train for the West on June 10, 1949. This locomotive is one of a large class introduced in 1911 and which, with several variations in detail, totalled 217.

Below right: The up Saturdays only 8.35am Falmouth-Paddington through restaurant car express (non-stop from Plymouth to London) passing Teignmouth station headed by 'Castle' class 4-6-0 No 4081 *Warwick Castle* on June 11, 1949.

Above: The up 10.45am Newton Abbot-Exeter (St Davids) stopping passenger train is a light load on Friday June 10. 1949 for Hawksworth 'County' class 4-6-0 No 1023 *County of Oxford* as it crosses Smugglers Lane footpath and stream bridge near Teignmouth

Below: Birmingham's Snow Hill station on Sunday September 13, 1953. 'Manor' Class 4-6-0 No 7810 *Draycott Manor* of Shrewsbury MPD is in charge of an up Class H through freight

Above right: '5101' class Collett
2-6-2T No 5106 piloting 'Castle'
class 4-6-0 No 7002 *Devizes
Castle* into Snow Hill station with
the ECS of an up excursion on
Sunday September 13, 1953.

Below right: '5700' class
0-6-0PT No 5738, a Stourbridge
MPD Locomotive, heads a Class
K stopping freight train through
Birmingham Snow Hill station on
the hazy morning of September
14, 1953.

Above left: Old Oak Common
MPD's 'Castle' class 4-6-0
No 7032 *Denbigh Castle* draws
away from platform 6 at
Birmingham Snow Hill station
with the Sunday 11.10am from
Paddington to Chester and
Birkenhead, on September 13,
1953.

Below left: '5101' class 2-6-2T
No 5184 leaves Snow Hill with
the 12.20pm stopping train to
Leamington Spa on September
13, 1953.

Above: Modified 'Hall' 4-6-0 No 6974 *Bryngwyn Hall,* an Old Oak Common MPD 'maid-of-all-work', heads up the gradient from the tunnels towards Snow Hill station, Birmingham, with an up Class H through freight for the south on Sunday September 13, 1953.

Below: '6100' class 2-6-2T No 6134 draws through the middle road at Snow Hill station Birmingham with empty coaching stock (a Birmingham-Torquay and Paignton set) on the same 1953 Sunday.

Above: Hawksworth '1500' class 0-6-0PT No 1502 of 1949, a short-wheelbase heavy shunting locomotive, is caught on the main line near Kennington Junction trundling a down Class K freight towards Hinksey yard alongside a local backwater of the River Isis, on Saturday July 18, 1953.

Below: The up 12.47pm Hereford-Paddington express at the Abingdon Road Bridge, Hinksey, South Oxford, is headed by Wolverhampton (Stafford Road) MPD-based Hawksworth 'County' class 4-6-0 No 1019 *County of Merioneth* on Friday, July 17 1953. The Hinksey yard 'gridiron' is off the goods road passing through the single-track extension to the otherwise graceful GWR design of overbridge.

Left: The southbound 8.42am Wolverhampton (Low Level)-Portsmouth Harbour 'Holiday Express' — a Saturdays only seasonal train, passes Hinksey yard, Oxford, headed by 'Hall' class 4-6-0 No 5960 *Saint Edmond Hall* on July 18, 1953

Below: Collett push-and-pull fitted '5400' class 0-6-0PT No 5413 has just cleared the Godstow Road Bridge near Wolvercote Junction with the down 2.50pm Oxford to Blenheim & Woodstock branch train on Wednesday July 15, 1953.

Above: The westbound 1.30pm Sheffield (Victoria)-Cardiff through train near Kennington Junction, south of Oxford. It has travelled via Nottingham (Victoria) and Woodford Halse to Banbury, where the locomotive change was usually made, and is now headed by 'Castle' class 4-6-0 No 5009 *Shrewsbury Castle* on Saturday July 18, 1953. Note the ex-NER brake first on Gresley bogies leading the train.

Below: The up 2.02pm Fairford-Oxford branch train rattles over the diamonds at Wolvercote Junction as it joins the Banbury line on Wednesday, July 15, 1953. It is headed by 0-6-0PT No 7412.

Above left: Seen at the Abingdon Road overbridge, Hinksey, near Oxford, is the up 7.45am Hereford-Paddington express headed by gleaming Worcester 'Castle' class 4-6-0 No 7005 *Lamphey Castle* on Saturday July 18, 1953. Much later, in August 1957, this locomotive was renamed *Sir Edward Elgar* in honour of the centenary of the birth of the composer.

Above right: 'Hall' class 4-6-0 No 5943 *Elmdon Hall* in BR lined green livery, from Worcester MPD, is passing Stratford-upon-Avon West Junction signalbox with the 4.20pm Leamington Spa-Worcester (Shrub Hill) on Saturday April 5, 1952. This train travelled via Honeybourne station using the direct Worcester line curve at Honeybourne Junction.

Below right: 'Castle' class 4-6-0 No 7007 *Great Western* — so renamed in January 1948 to mark the fact that this was the last express passenger locomotive built by the GWR (it was previously named *Ogmore Castle*). The transfers of the GWR coat of arms, seen on the centre splasher in the photograph, were applied to both splashers a little later than the renaming. No 7007 is passing the Oxford reservoirs, in Hinksey Park, with the up 11.00am Hereford-Paddington express on Friday, July 17, 1953.

Above right: The down 4.45pm Paddington-Hereford express near Kennington Junction, south of Oxford on Saturday, July 18 1953 headed by 'Castle' class 4-6-0 No 5086 *Viscount Horne.* Another shining example of Worcester MPD's artistry with the cleaning rags.

Above left: 'Hall' class 4-6-0 No 5960 *Saint Edmund Hall* returning from Portsmouth with the 3.30pm Portsmouth Harbour—Wolverhampton through train on Saturday July 18, 1953. It is seen between the signals near Kennington Junction, Oxford.

Below left: An unidentified down excursion, a smart rake of stock in uniform carmine-and-cream livery, approaching Wolvercote Junction from the Oxford direction at Port Meadows. Motive power is 'Hall' class 4-6-0 No 5900 *Hinderton Hall* reasonably clean in BR lined black livery on Monday July 13, 1953.

Above: A Sunday engineering working at Birmingham Snow Hill station. '9000' class 4-4-0 No 9001, a 'Dukedog' (built in 1936 incorporating parts from a 1906 4-4-0), is leaving the down main platform, heading a Class C express ballast train to Oswestry on September 13, 1953.

Below: A view inside one of the two roundhouses at St Philips Marsh MPD, Bristol on Sunday August 19, 1951. Locomotives in this little group are, left to right: '5600' class 0-6-2T No 6656 (at home); '9000' class 4-4-0 No 9011 (a visitor from Swindon MPD); and again at home, '5700' class 0-6-0 pannier tank No 4624.

Above: Chester MPD-based 'Hall' class 4-6-0 No 5994 *Roydon Hall* making a sure-footed start from Shrewsbury on the down Sunday afternoon Chester and Birkenhead express on April 27, 1952 (probably the 11.10am from Paddington). *Roydon Hall* was a Swindon product of 1939.

Below: Cross-London transfer freight — the up 12.50pm Old Oak-Lambeth with a clear road through Olympia station; '5700' class 0-6-0PT No 4698 is in charge on Saturday October 6, 1951.

Left: Maunsell 'Lord Nelson' class 4-6-0 No 30859 *Lord Duncan*— an 'odd man out' in the class, being the solitary locomotive fitted in 1929 with driving wheels experimentally reduced to 6ft 3in dia from the standard 6ft 7in dia of the remainder of the class. It is passing Battledown flyover with the down 9.30am Waterloo-Bournemouth West express on August 4, 1951.

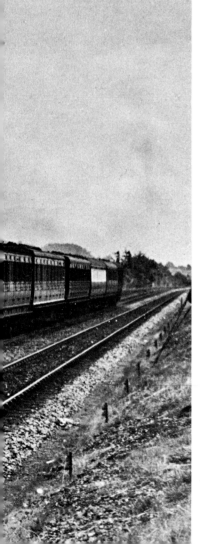

Above: Viewed from the footbridge at Salisbury station, from a point above the former GWR Westbury line platforms, Bulleid 'Battle of Britain' class 4-6-2 No 34052 *Lord Dowding* leaves the station with an up train for Waterloo from Ilfracombe on Sunday April 25, 1954.

Left: Maunsell Class U 2-6-0 No 31624, based at Guildford MPD, heads past the Worting cottages with an unidentified Salisbury line train, possibly the Saturdays only 10.27am Waterloo-Andover Junction running late, on July 21, 1951.

Left: A truly LBSC design at the home of the LBSC on Sunday, October 5, 1952 — Marsh Class H2 4-4-2 No 32424 *Beachy Head,* one of six locomotives built in 1911-12. The Atlantic is waiting at Brighton station for all passengers to get back on board a return RCTS Pullman Special for Victoria, via the Quarry line.

Below: The down 9.00am London (Victoria)-Dover/Ostend Continental express in the widened chalk cutting at Knockholt station. 'Merchant Navy' class 4-6-2 No 35025 *Brocklebank Line* attacks the 1 in 170 gradient on Saturday March 31, 1951.

Right: BR Standard 'Britannia' class 4-6-2 No 70009 *Alfred the Great* passing Battledown flyover with the down 12.30pm 'Bournemouth Belle' Pullman express from Waterloo on August 4, 1951.

Below: 'Lord Nelson' class 4-6-0 No 30863 *Lord Rodney* is awaiting departure from Oxford on the 8.37am Newcastle-Bournemouth West cross-country express, having just relieved an ex GWR locomotive on Tuesday, July 14 1953.

Right: Maunsell 'Eastleigh Arthur' Class N15 4-6-0 No 30450 *Sir Kay,* one of a batch of five locomotives introduced in 1925 with detail alterations and increased weight. It leans to the curve at Battledown flyover with an up West of England express, believed to be the 8.00am from Ilfracombe, on August 4, 1951.

Below: The up 8.35am Bournemouth West-Waterloo buffet car express at Esher on Saturday November 11, 1950, headed by Bulleid 'Battle of Britain' class 4-6-2 No 34109 *Sir Trafford Leigh-Mallory* in the experimental dark blue livery with Southern-type horizontal lining.

Above: The down 10.54am Waterloo-Salisbury semi-fast is passing Esher headed by Maunsell 'Lord Nelson' class 4-6-0 No 30850 *Lord Nelson* on Saturday November 11, 1950. The stock is in carmine and cream livery, by now universally applied on all Regions.

Above: A locomotive beautifully polished for a special occasion is ex-LSWR Adams Class 0415 4-4-2T No 30583 — a 'radial tank' to most Southern folk. The design was introduced in 1882. No 30583 is departing from Exmouth station on April 12, 1953 at the head of the 2.55pm Ian Allan 'Branch Special' run on that Sunday visit by train from London.

Left: Maunsell Class U 2-6-0 No 31796 is threading the road bridge at the eastern end of Exeter Central station on April 12, 1953 with the down 1.40pm Salisbury-Plymouth (Friary) stopping train.

Right: The South Hayling scene. Stroudley ex-LB & SCR Class A1X 0-6-0T No 32677 from Fratton MPD stands at the Island's terminus, South Hayling station after arrival with the branch train from Havant on Saturday May 29, 1954. Introduced as Class A1 in 1872, the class was from 1911 rebuilt by Marsh to Class A1X by the provision of new boilers with extended smokeboxes.

Below: Drummond LSWR-designed Class D15 4-4-0 No 30465 is about to pass the high girders of Battledown flyover on August 4, 1951 with the 8.42am Wolverhampton to Portsmouth Harbour via Oxford, Reading West and Basingstoke.

Above: At Walton-on-Thames station, the down 11.54am three-coach Waterloo-Salisbury stopping train is headed by Bulleid blue-liveried 'Merchant Navy' Class 4-6-2 No 35006 *Peninsular & Oriental SN Co* on November 11, 1950.

Above right: One of the 'Schools' class locomotives left in the condition of the original Maunsell design, as introduced to the Southern Railway in 1930. Class V 4-4-0 No 30932 *Blundells* is standing at Radstock (Somerset & Dorset Railway section of the Southern Region) piloting Fowler Class 2P 4-4-0 No 40601 at the head of an Ian Allan *Trains Illustrated* excursion en route for Bath, Green Park, on Sunday April 25, 1954.

Below right: The up 10.40am Basingstoke-Waterloo semi-fast, a neat carmine-and-cream liveried train, is headed by Urie 'Arthur' Class N15 4-6-0 No 30743 *Lyonnesse* in green livery through Esher on November 11, 1950.

Above: Maunsell 'Scottish Arthur' Class N15 4-6-0 No 30782 *Sir Brian* from Eastleigh MPD (71A) heads the 8.27am Newcastle-Oxford Bournemouth West express towards Kennington Junction, Oxford on July 18, 1953.

Below: 'Lord Nelson' No 30863 *Lord Rodney* is passing Hinksey Park reservoirs, South Oxford, with the southbound 9.20am Birkenhead (Woodside)-Bournemouth West express which it had taken over at Oxford on Friday, July 17 1953

Above left: A 'bob-tail' at Kensington Olympia station, London-Kirtley ex-LC&DR auto-train fitted Class R 0-4-4T No 31660, introduced in 1891/2 but later rebuilt with an H class boiler. It is seen leaving the station with the up 12.36pm Post Office special, Kensington to Clapham Junction, on Saturday October 6, 1951. It is passing the typically L&NWR Kensington South main signalbox and signals. On the up through line opposite, ex-GWR Collett 5700 class 0-6-0PT No 7791 waits for the road with a Class F inter-Regional transfer freight.

Above right: A combined operation here and poor light in which to work! O. S. Nock is footplating Class E1 4-4-0 No 31504 on the down 11.50am Victoria-Dover (Priory) on Saturday October 31, 1953. It is seen near Ravensbourne. The Stewarts Lane MPD staff have managed a nice polish on the E1.

Below left: Maunsell Class W 2-6-4T No 31911, one of a class of 15 locomotives which were introduced to the Southern in 1931, is slowly moving through Kensington Olympia station with an up Class H through transfer freight from north of the Thames to a Southern Region yard on October 6, 1951.

Below right: The Dover portion of the down 8.35am from London, Victoria at Sittingbourne. It is headed by Maunsell Class L1 4-4-0 No 31788 from Ramsgate MPD. Also seen in this photograph of Tuesday, November 14 1950 are Wainwright Class H 0-4-4T No 31308 on the connecting Sheerness train and Class C 0-6-0 No 31268, also a Wainwright ex-SE&C design.

The down 10.50am 'Atlantic Coast Express' from Waterloo is passing Raynes Park and going well, in the charge of Bulleid 'Merchant Navy' Class 4-6-2 No 35010 *Blue Star*. The date is September 23, 1950.